better together*

*This book is best read together, grownup and kid.

a
kids
book
about

a kids book about

COMMUNITY

by Shane Feldman

**a
kids
book
about**™

A Kids Book About books are available online:
www.akidsbookabout.com

To share your stories, ask questions, or inquire about bulk
purchases (schools, libraries, and nonprofits), please use
the following email address:

hello@akidsbookabout.com

ISBN: 978-1-951253-65-3

Designed by Rick DeLucco
Edited by Denise Morales Soto

To my mom, who taught me that parenting is a practice of unconditional love, acceptance, and support.

Intro

Without a sense of community, is it possible to experience life to the fullest?

Each of us wants to feel seen, heard, and valued. The thing is, that sense of community we all crave doesn't just happen by default. The active practice of reaching out and sharing meaningful experiences with others is what saved me from a downward spiral of loneliness and isolation. I only wish I had learned to incorporate this practice as a kid so I could have avoided years of pain and hurt.

I wrote this book as an antidote to loneliness. It's a simple little guide for kids to make more quality friendships and live a life full of joy, excitement, and ease with less sadness, frustration, and heartbreak.

This book is here to help every kid identify and spark that sense of community in their own life. It may seem mysterious at first, but it's actually quite simple. Like anything, it just takes a bit of practice.

What is

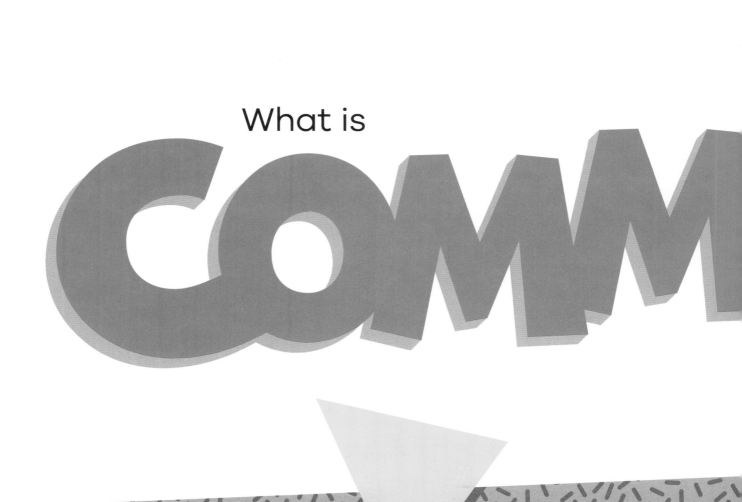

Some people think that
community is where you live.

Others think community
is a group of people.

There are even some who think
community is who you are.

My name is

SHANE,

and I want to tell you
what community
means to me.

Community is about
sharing something
important to you
with other people.

Maybe **1** person, or **2**,
or **10**, or even **100!**

It's something I've spent
my whole life learning about...

mostly because
when I was growing up,
I never felt like I was part of one.

Once, during the summer,
I moved to a brand new city.

I was really excited, but also
really nervous.

EXCITED
because this move meant
a whole new adventure

and **NERVOUS**
because that new adventure
meant a new school.

A new school where I had no friends and no one knew who I was.
Not the kids, not the teachers—

NO ONE.

I FELT ALONE BEFORE
I EVEN GOT THERE.

The first day of school was
even harder than I thought
it was going to be.

I didn't know where
my classroom was.

I had nobody to talk to.

And the teachers didn't
even say my name right.

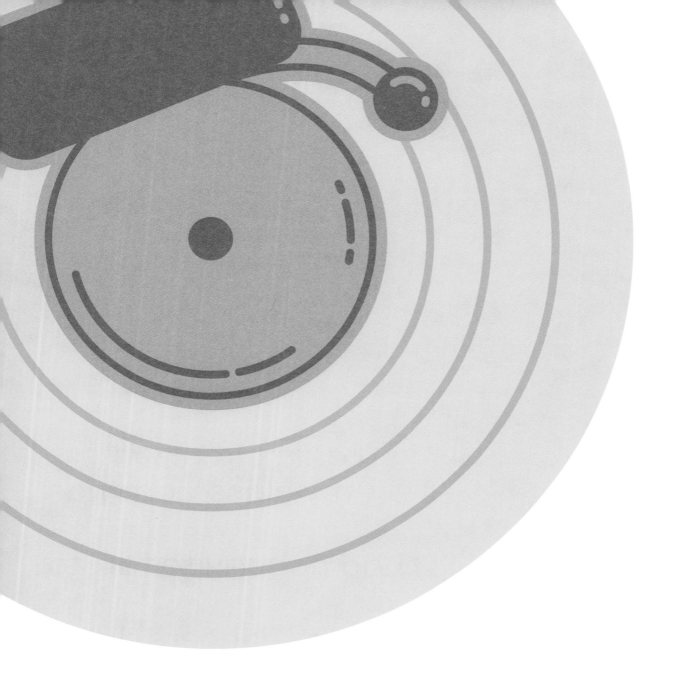

Then the worst part
of the day was right after
the lunch bell rang.

The whole school poured into the hallways and everything got really loud and busy.

Everyone broke out into groups and stood together in circles, laughing and talking, and I was the only kid by myself.

I WAS ALL ALONE.

At that moment,
I thought I wasn't a part
of the community.

That I was on the
OUTSIDE
and they were on the
INSIDE.

I thought that community was something you were either part of or you weren't.

I thought community happened for some people (the lucky ones) and not the rest of us.

But later I learned that's not the way community works at all.

Community doesn't happen like magic.

It's actually something we get to build.

That's right,
you and I have
the power to build

COMMUNITY!

Remember,
we said community is about
sharing experiences.

It's the difference between:

READING A BOOK ALONE OR

READING A BOOK WITH FRIENDS.

PLAYING PRETEND BY YOURSELF OR

GOING OUTSIDE AND PLAYING TAG WITH THE OTHER KIDS.

DOODLING BY YOURSELF IN YOUR ROOM OR

DRAWING WITH CHALK ON THE SIDEWALK WITH YOUR NEIGHBORS.

EATING BY YOURSELF IN YOUR ROOM OR

EATING WITH YOUR FAMILY INSTEAD.

By the way,
this doesn't mean you
always have to do everything
with someone else.

It's **OK** to be by
yourself sometimes.

I'm an introverted person, which means I **NEED** extra time by myself or I can get tired and cranky.

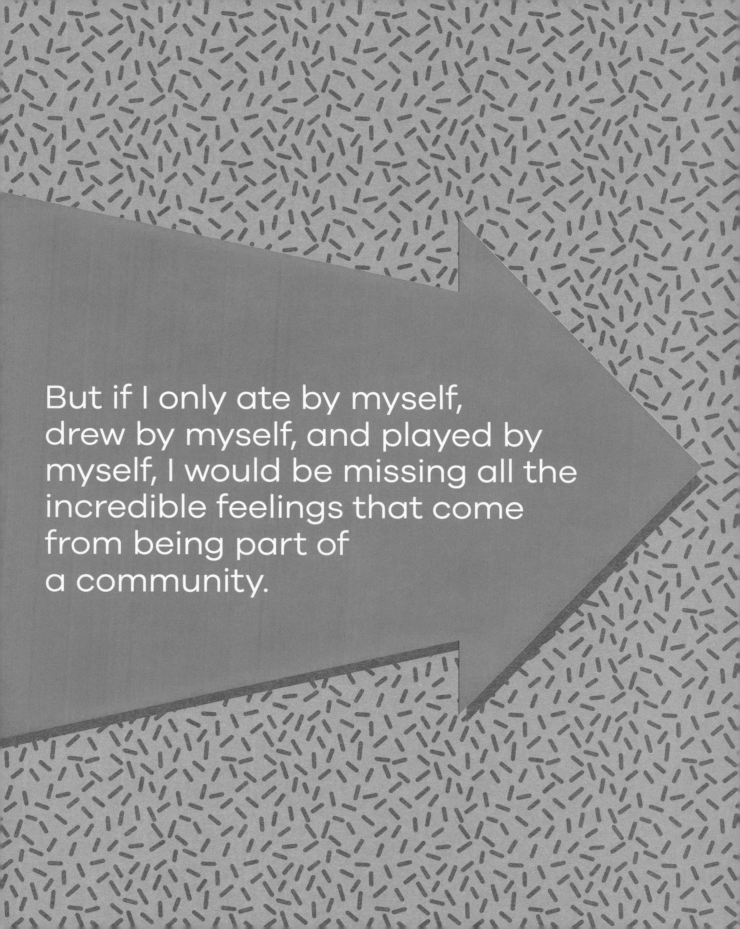

But if I only ate by myself, drew by myself, and played by myself, I would be missing all the incredible feelings that come from being part of a community.

FEELINGS LIKE...

- ⭐ joy
- ⭐ fulfillment
- ⭐ love
- ⭐ inspiration
- ⭐ fun
- ⭐ pride
- ⭐ helpfulness
- ⭐ creativity
- ⭐ satisfaction
- ⭐ surprise
- ⭐ relief
- ⭐ comfort
- ⭐ confidence
- ⭐ support
- ⭐ empowerment

(JUST TO NAME A FEW.)

There are so many good things about community and you can find it...

ANYW

There are even different types of communities.

Some that you discover...

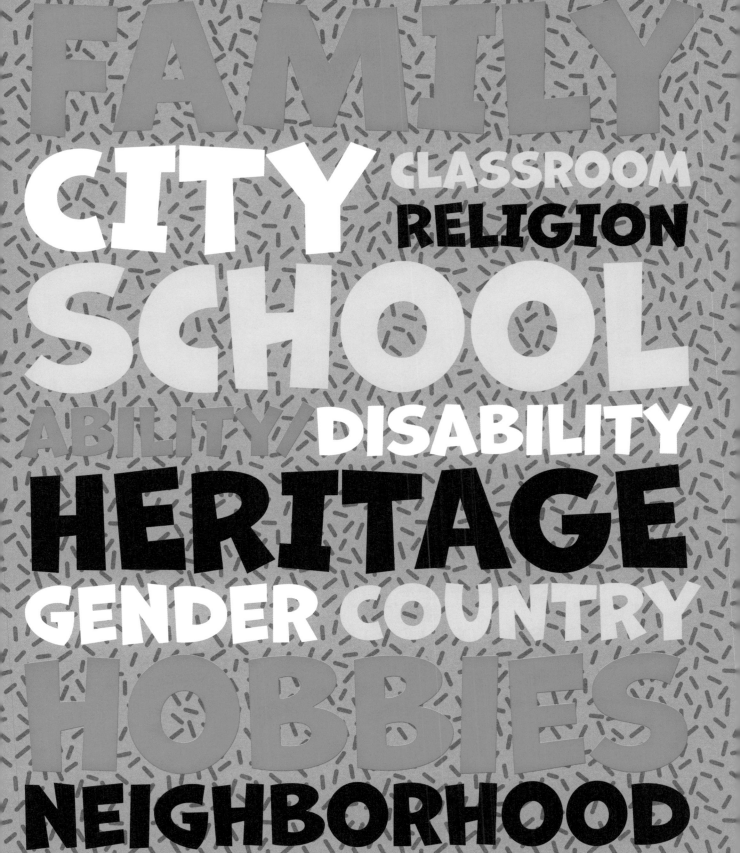

FAMILY
CITY CLASSROOM
RELIGION
SCHOOL
ABILITY/ DISABILITY
HERITAGE
GENDER COUNTRY
HOBBIES
NEIGHBORHOOD

And some that you create.

SITTING WITH
SOMEONE AT LUNCH
MULTI-PLAYER
GAMING
VOLUNTEERING
PLAYING A NEW SPORT
PERFORMING
IN THE SCHOOL PLAY
JOINING THE
SCIENCE FAIR

When I started at my new school,
I felt like an outsider.

I wanted to feel
part of a community,
but the problem was
I didn't know what my
community was.

SO I TRIED THEM ALL!

First, I tried

SOCCER.

That wasn't for me.

Next, I tried the

SCIENCE TEAM

and didn't really enjoy that either.

Then I tried the

ART

CLUB,

that was actually pretty fun!

There I met other kids
that liked a lot of the
same things I did.

That was my community,
and once I found it,
I felt so much less alone.

My new school didn't
seem so scary anymore.

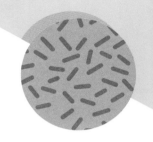

Sometimes finding and creating communities can take a while, but other times, it happens right away.

One time I asked to join
a group of kids who were
playing a game...

They said yes!

COMMUNITY!

Community can even happen by accident.

I was watching kids
play basketball one time
and the ball bounced
over to me.

When I picked it up,
they asked me
if I wanted to play.

I didn't think basketball
was my community,
but turns out, it was!

The more I started trying new things,
the more communities I was joining.

I thought I wasn't part of any community, but it turns out I was actually part of lots of different ones.

I just didn't know it yet.

Can you think of any
communities you belong to?

Either ones you've discovered
or ones you've created?

How about one
you want to create?

The good news is
there's no rule about
how many communities
you can be part of.

Be a part of **10**,
100, even **1,000**...

it's up to you!

Your communities can also change over time.

They don't have to stay the same.

BUT THE ONE THING I WANT YOU TO REMEMBER IS THIS:

Once you close this book,
I want you to know
that you're more connected
than you think.

That you are a part
of a community.

And you can be a part
of so many more.

So the next time you're doing something fun...

Maybe reading a book you love (like this one),

watching a great movie,

or playing a fun game...

I want you to try to share that experience with others.

Even with just one person.

THAT'S TH

PLACE TO

HE BEST
D START.

Outro

It's easy to be mystified by community, connection, and friendship. For many kids, it seems like these are reserved for the special few. The lucky ones.

But not anymore.

Community doesn't happen by magic—it's actually something we get to build. And now, you know exactly how to start building that community in your own life, which means the road ahead is only going to get brighter and more enriching.

Now is your opportunity to help that amazing kid in your life feel the genuine connection that we all crave. That sense of community is what activates the leadership qualities within us all. It allows us to think and act as our best selves, and that goes for us grownups too!

Kids are natural community builders, but sometimes they need help understanding where to start. With you behind them cheering them on, they're going to be a true community builder before you know it.

find more kids books about

autism, addiction, diversity, sexual abuse, immigration, gender, suicide, adoption, climate change, voting, and technology.

 akidsbookabout.com

share
your read*

*Tell somebody, post a photo, or give this book away to share what you care about.

@akidsbookabout